QUENTIN S. CRISP

OCTOBER

SNUGGLY BOOKS

Just being alive,
As usual. I only
Remember having
Been this one person. Yet I
Am life. And I'm hungover.

Mornington Terrace.
Morning. Rain on paving stones.
Through the area
Window, a table in a
Basement flat—a passing glimpse.

Ferns at the window,
Like an early photograph.
A little courtyard
Of rain and hydrangeas. Time
Should not pass here, but it does.

For this rain never
To end. The only kind of
Immortality
I want. Apart from that, no
Events, each needing the next.

Now the rain has stopped,
Stripy spiral of a snail
Stretching slow along
The leaf of a hydrangea,
Horns faintly waving, sensing.

Study continues
To be an excavation
Of my ignorance.
Meanwhile, I present the world
This: my poetic thesis.

Troubled yesterday
By many things, but mostly
By the nightmare sense
That bad things preponderate.
The riddle: we carry on.

I did not enjoy
Chateaubriand, but I was
Moved by Brendan's words:
"I love Chateaubriand." So
Shines the light from distant stars.

I felt the shining
Admiration, pity, grief
I feel when I have
Said or done a thing that I
Realise might be hurtful.

What to be said on
The question of success? Quoth
Goethe and Bacon:
"Success—the thief of freedom!"
I read their lament—who mine?

Never comes in waves.
The knowledge, or, as it were,
The fear like knowledge
That I will never succeed.
Again—never overcome.

A woman teaching
A young boy to cross the road:
A custom we don't
Question anymore because
We decided we need cars.

Who is cis? We fail
To see each life as something
To be realised—
A species of one. We make
Imitation into law.

Pouring green tea by
My unlined refill pad, I
See a liquid spot
Appear, like watercolour,
Recall paper-peaceful times.

Condensation on
My windows this morning. For
The first time since spring,
I have the heater on, but
Open windows, too, for air.

Exhausted. Childless
By choice and fate. Bothered by
An instinct confirmed
By Plotinus: Creation
Is superfluous to God.

It's okay. It's not
Okay. Both of them end in
'So what?' I concur
When Lewis concludes, battles
Need grounds, so dual's out, too.

Gratuitous. That's
The word I'm looking for. No,
I'm not the first to
Find it. Freedom. Gratitude.
Beautiful contingency.

And I see in these
Fallen oak and horse chestnut
Leaves, C.S. Lewis
Seeing the same thing, plain as
English grammar: God's relief.

A grey veil obscures
The almost forgotten thing
We supposed life was.
And why? Because we seem bound
To a meaningless decline.

Yet, supposedly,
We believe in Hell no more.
Spufford promises
Even Christians say it's gone.
Is it only in my eye?

Will they open Hell
Up to tourists, now it can't
Support itself? Build
A virtual Hell? Campaign? "Hell:
Damned if you do, and damned if . . ."

Impressionable,
I pander and feel shame. Then
Again, when I am
Forthright, confidence betrays
Me. How hard, simplicity.

Watching Booker White
Play guitar recently, it
Came to me, the blues
Represents how I want to
Write: keeping on, transcending.

The electronic
Loop of an alarm takes on
A double meaning.
You force yourself from bed, drink
Coffee, nervous, comforted.

Warm, starchy socks and
The weekday morning cold floor
Impart a merry
Tingle not just physical
But of life's untold goodness.

The Bubba Gump shrimp—
A plush magnet on my fridge.
When I move I'll take
It with me; when I die—what
A sad object it will be!

His insight into
Human character, Joshi
Says, is insightful.
Everyone trying to sound
Like they know something; failing.

Still, there are havens
For those who deplore what is
Done to language and
The world. Quiet and a page
Of well-tooled meditations.

I ordered Anselm's
Major Works (Oxford Classics)
From the Open Book
On King Street. How long will they
Allow such things to exist?

Stairs descend around
An old, caged lift-shaft, empty.
The office. Evening
Comes here, fatalistic, soft.
This unnoticed work, then death.

Reflection rather
Than reaction. Once, not to
Speak was to support
The pollution of our minds
By media. Now, to speak.

As I talked to John,
It came to me: in Chômu
We've done a good thing,
But only a few dryads
Of the written word will know.

The smell of coal dust
In autumn: is it real, or
A ghost wink between
World and mind? No one knows what
It means to me. I won't tell.

Writers till the last
Century, cry poor like this:
"I was down to three
Servants." At least they could write.
Their equivalents today?

Why, last night, did I
Especially remember
Mrs Kurita
Trying to find a parking
Space on our Kusatsu trip?

The darkness, last night,
So complete. What do I mean
By that? It was not
Entirely black. There were lights.
Yet it was closed, timeless, cold.

I wanted to put
Seventeen Seconds on, back
At the flat. Instead,
I found Crescent. Perfect. So,
What's going on in Bristol?

How to make the most
Of home (by which I mean, this
Flat)? Stare at a pack
Of Anadin. My glasses
Rest on *Kafū the Scribbler.*

A particular
Waterlogged smell, like dog drool,
Makes me think of drowned
Grass at the edge of a school
Sports field. A provincial smell.

All the more because
Automation, A.I. and
Dubious boons of
This kind, promise to make our
Problems, or us, obsolete.

All the more, in this
Dark night, in this English soil,
In the riddles of
The Exeter Book, I feel,
There must be a truer dream.

We grow wide of who
We think we are and keep on
Going. No one can
Tolerate this. Yet, no one
Stops it. Expanding. Dying.

The universe is
A crucifixion, arms spread.
If it's meaningless,
Why would it stop? Meaningful?
We can't imagine, and yet . . .

Rain thickens, passes.
I breathe, and I will cease. If
I fear death, I must
Save the universe. From what?
Spiralling into itself.

"... and similar droll
Comments," said Bee-chan. "Droll is
Such a good word," said
Rebs. "Yes it is." In my heart
I concurred, and made a third.

I fictionalise.
For me, it's fundamental.
What if fiction were
Removed from the human brain?
That would make a good story.

Say all problems were
Eliminated and there
Were only carpet
Warehouses and Sundays; once
In a thousand years, I'd smile.

What I'm saying is,
Maybe Christmas-everyday-
In-Heaven's not so
Bad. Maybe a thin smile now
And then justifies the whole.

There is no use for
Colour in a universe
Of good, evil and
Salvation. What is the world,
Then, if more than a chessboard?

I can't even grasp
My own thoughts, yet I'm asked to
Grasp the possible
Future end as if it were
A certainty and stop it.

Eliminating
The ego: not serious.
Scorning sentiment:
Not serious. Only to
See everything, real, unique.

I'm almost sure my
Plant attempted suicide.
It tugged itself off
The windowsill weeks back, since
When its leaves drop mortally.

The same despair that
Has sacked the world, we take for
A solution: kill
Ourselves and let the planet
Heal. No. We have work to do.

The answer? You won't
Like it. There are those who would
Build the temple and
There are those who would prefer
The temple should not be built.

Films, songs and so on
Are poignant because we can
Replay a moment;
We can't replay our lives. My
'Green scarf period' just goes.

I'm more concerned with
The ground of being than with
Heaven. So mock me
A jot more accurately—
Use '*soil*-fairies', not '*sky-*'.

Another Rosebud
Memory comes unprompted
After decades of
Not. Me stepping on puffballs
In the fields round Berry Down.

I had a welling
Urge to read Murnane again—
That rapturous sense
Of being on a threshold.
But no—I want to step through.

Murnane's racing stones
Line up at the threshold to
His garden, about
To jump through and race, he says.
It's magic. When will it start?

Than magic, nothing
More important, and nothing
Less here, less now, and
So I despair of the worth
Of my life's work. Or of life.

Dominika and
I spoke the word 'vora' at
The same time, meaning
One of endless thresholds. I
Must look up Plato's 'hora'.

Some people despair
The way politicians kiss
Babies. It's merely
The world. And politics is
Another kind of gossip.

Why do you require
Me to be horrified in
The seconds before
I die? Truth? If there's truth now,
There's truth, too, after I'm dead.

Never as cold these
Days as when I was small, but
With socks drying on
The oil heater as the sky
Grows light, some of that cold's warmth.

This morning I changed
Both trousers and coat. Now, at
The station, I find
I'm bereft of tissues to
Wipe my nose. Strange discomfort.

Again, not yet dead.
Again, still alive. Today,
In the world of things,
I might once more waste time on
Facebook, buy crisps, play with words.

For "play with words", I
Might have written "write to" or
"Hang out with friends," and
'Things' link endlessly between
Sleep in the eye and Anselm.

Ligotti's good at
Titles: *The Conspiracy
Against the Human
Race.* Yes. But it's a human
Conspiracy. It's your choice.

The conspiracy's
First blow was against faith, then
The human soul; now
Humanity itself must
Fall. Dominoes of hubris.

I can't imagine
A mind blind to transcendence,
Yet plenty deny.
I saw colours then read of
Them. Do they read and not see?

Paul Foot's tale: the girl
Drowned, jeered by rich folk hogging
The lifeboat. Jesus
Said she would live; she died. She
Was mad. Was she a loser?

Thinking how small, how
Infinitesimal, my
Attempt, I recall
Mister God, This is Anna.
How eclectically I've read.

My smallness comforts
Rather than troubles me, like
The finite, precious
Illuminated letter,
Found, lost, in infinity.

"Only, I forgot."—
Matt Johnson on the secret
Of the universe.
Does the secret need us to
Remember it? Cloudy day.

Ligotti's 'Drapeau'—
There is one world, strange through lack
Of strangeness. Rainy
Red and green neon. Frankie
& Benny's. Bexleyheath night.

I saw a picture
Of a woman. I don't know
The background. It haunts
Me. Disfigured by violence.
Evil imprinted on flesh.

The question: how can
We overcome this evil?
This force that believes
Because it conquers matter,
It conquers also spirit.

I have no answer,
So I fear that Hell awaits
(For me). This despite
The protestations of both
Atheists and Christians.

Now I think of it,
Anselm was my entry to
Philosophy, at
A-level. Round the same time,
Bob Dwight lent me Sartre's *Words*.

Egg-fried rice. The smell
Fills the entry hall again,
Coming from a flat
Upstairs. A thrill of contrast—
Bright against the cold outside.

Shadwell Station. One
Section of the tunnel gapes
Dripping to the air.
Rain spills on the underground
Tracks, platforms, benches there.

That it is not what
I expected, but that it
Intelligibly is—
The ordinary texture,
Is-level, of supreme good.

Stories seem simple
As childhood—dunces within
The school of I.Q.
Darwinism. Yet they step
Back and include everything.

Another morning
Going home to work. New Cross.
I get on a train
And let a pigeon off. It
Seems unsure. Is this its stop?

Just now, the darkest
Clouds I've ever seen, sagging
Like collapsing stars.
In the time it took to fetch
My camera—darkburst, rainfall.

So all things fall through;
Condense in the atmosphere,
Then precipitate.
As there's nothing I can do,
I should come undone. Pull through.

The death penalty
In one case—for drivers who
Splash you in passing.
I broke my umbrella in
Anger, trying to close it.

History's a fog
Of contingency. We learn
Of the accidents.
We come to dwell in them. 'Dwell'
Means 'to live', its root, 'to stray'.

I'll be gone all too
Soon. What will I miss in and
What will I leave to
This bottomless hourglass
Whorl of work, winks and warfare?

Did Suggs plan that voice,
Deadpan against a tight and
Playful two-tone band?
When I was young these things came
As if always fully formed.

A pessimist? No,
Not really. All I want is,
When the scientists
Fuck the world up for us, that
I can say, "I told you so."

Tidying. Folding
A clean sheet and putting it
In the cupboard. Where
Can I buy mothballs these days?
Suddenly, I am inspired.

Am I more selfish,
Or less self-important? I
Find the wish for fame
Receding; the wish to let
The world go hang, increasing.

Sometimes these days I
Feel I'm on the wrong side of
History, the wrong
Side of Heaven and Hell. Of
Buddhism. What a relief.

Perhaps every day,
I wish that existence would
Gently let me go.
Why am I forced to atone
For its vain controversies?

I read a review
Of *It's a Wonderful Life*.
"It almost persuades
Us," said the reviewer. Why
Have children if it doesn't?

Elms were threatened. Now
They're okay, the papers say.
Now horse chestnuts are
Endangered. By the larvae
Of a moth, and by chainsaws.

Horse chestnut branches
Have a tendency to fall,
It seems, and people
Don't like this. A branch crashing
To the ground. What poetry!

All that straining to
Be as straight as a stranger's
Ruler. I'm crooked
As the Useless Tree, merry
With rain and mad with disease.

Sycamore seeds on
Pavements. Walking with Bee-chan
At night. I felt that
Childhood story-sense I've felt
And failed to name so often.

It surprises me
England has the power, still,
To cast such spells. It's
What I want to die into,
All Masefield, mulled wine and wolves.

A dull afternoon.
Frying mushrooms in garlic.
A slow, celluloid
Sizzle like an old film reel,
Projecting, simply, my life.

Thursday, 20th

That this isn't real
(Compared, say, to God), but that
It's everything (since
God is everywhere)—I find
This the paradox most fudged.

That this isn't real
(Compared, say, to God), but that
It's everything—this
Is the paradox I must
Face—the paradox most fudged.

I want to address
This whole question of self. It's
All very worthy
To say, "I don't exist," but
Think of a friend: who is it?

I keep thinking of
Richmond Green, as if it were
A site of eerie
Happiness, otherworldly
Reunion, elfin truth.

I return to this
After ethics, survival,
Struggles with reason.
It pales them like a greater
Good—a snatch of fairy song.

Though no one ever
Heard that song from beginning
To end; though no one
Knows where it comes from, or if
It can be followed. Or should.

For me this strangeness
Is not flavourless. Strange, too,
How Socrates or
Buddha—the greatest minds—left
This for others to explore.

It seems unchristian,
But then, Lewis seemed to know
Of it; Narnia
Is drenched in it. In my soul,
Bindweed blooms, dew-gemmed with it.

Anselm says there is
A "natural language", formed of
Ideas in God's
Mind. To find the natural words for
The fairy song—my life's work.

I'd like to propose
A fallacy. To Chuang Tzu's
Question they reply,
"But we know butterflies don't
Dream." The Earthling Fallacy.

Green tea caffeine? Or
Nerves, perhaps? A half-pleasant
Tingle of unease.
It's morning and once more, I
Must face the rest of my life.

When nihilism
Asks, 'Why?', there's nothing to stop
Us replying, 'Why
Not?'; Why not assume this 'Why?'
Crops ever up through *telos*?

They want to preserve
The meaning of sneering at
Meaning. *That*, they want
To preserve: without meaning
To sneer at meaning. Absurd!

Birds are twittering
And warbling today as if
It's spring. I recall
They did this, too, when it was
Almost spring. Always new starts.

A Barbara Windsor
Doll. All automated now.
Yet it expresses
Something. Message shaped by mind.
By whom for whom? Me, at least.

Everyone wants quick
Answers. If you don't commit
To a conclusion
Before you've reached it, they doubt
Your virtue—whose side you're on.

Change. You move here, to
London, to be near friends. They
Move away. Marriage
Or career. A tile puzzle
Of loneliness—that's the world.

Of course there are plans
To eliminate cash, so
They can keep better
Tabs on us. They'll sell it to
Us somehow, call it 'progress'.

Thus Facebook's promise
Is fulfilled: the maximum
Of loneliness and
Visibility combined
In a slick, locked-in design.

Conversations with
Goethe. The word 'important'
Recurs and I feel
Envious. Not because of
His status, but his era.

Writing this page, for
A moment I saw it looped
In a capsule of
Time, existing, little read,
Before humanity's end.

Stepping stones. To where?
What's more, they move beneath our
Feet. Why did we think
We could build a home, here in
Time, on sinking stepping stones?

As you grow older,
Those you know start to die. One
By one. Suddenly.
Slowly. We die trying to
Live. Our rulers simply die.

The mead-hall of Bede.
Firelight and warmth, not lasting.
Knowing to itself
Unknown. A traveller hears
Voices, stark against the night.

The thing I hate most
About people is they want
You to say, "I'm good,"
Before they'll believe that you're
Good. Naïve, mistrustful fools.

Tree trunks at night curve
Solid with shadow and cars'
Fearful headlights, like
Waking up from a nightmare
To life, not sure you're awake.

I can't help thinking,
If I love someone it's not
Because they're good, it's
Because they're who they are. But
'Law before love' has returned.

Before, rebels came
To overthrow the law and
Replace it with love.
What strange world is this where they
Come to replace love with law?

But we began it.
I recall Ligotti's words:
"With apologies
To The Beatles, it isn't
Love; all you need is justice."

An interest in
Fiction requires a sense of
Immortal youth and
A fear of body and soul's
Destruction, forever twinned.

Sometimes I feel my
Interest in fiction slide.
Entertainment is
Faith; the opposite almost
The case. What, then, is knowledge?

Freedom, yes, but not
That kind of freedom. Rules, yes,
But not that kind of
Rule. "You are a pedant and
I am a stickler." Who's who?

We thwart ourselves when
We beat our foes. Everyone
Has a right to be
Accepted, but what happens,
Then, to our right to reject?

The feeling, again,
Of satisfaction, just at
Being able to
Turn on the hot water tap.
The soul's daily solid ground.

So, one thing I'll miss
Is Triptykon. "Lie upon
Lie; mankind will die."
Is this paradox? Eros
Binds us to life with such lies.

Sustainable? For
How long? Not even the sun
Is sustainable.
All you have to do is live
And die. And now, October.

The cloudy patterns
Of the windows that look down
Upon the drainpipe
Courtyard. Tessellated brains.
Oh, in death I am broken.

Let each thing live and
Die, die and live in my brain's
Obscurity, dreams
Forgotten, leaving just this
Inevitable fossil.

I think of the sixth
Mass extinction and I try
To tidy my mind.
Or prove I've tortured myself.
We fight with the truth, we lose.

Like serene, soundless
Rotor blades on the scrap of
Lawn outside, the sun
In the cherry tree, leaf-shot
Into dazzling dapple.

A café. Behind
Me, a blind woman complained,
She and her husband
Had underpaid. "We're trying
To do the right thing." What grief!

Cosmopolitan.
Pagan. These are opposites.
Has the first, driving
Out the spirits of things, made
Us all materialists?

Materialists,
After all, are not those who
Value things. These we
Call animists. For later
Reference: 'ghosts of the earth'.

Following a lead,
I bought *As You Like It* with
A cover by Blake:
The wounded stag. So many
Pieces I must assemble.

Looking round my flat:
The warm outlines of objects,
Like a patina
Of my body oils. I can
Believe they live, as dreams do.

By now I should be
Preparing to die, but I've
Still not got my best
Work out. Rising too late too
Often, I've let myself down.

No one understands—
Really, no one—the pressure
To fail, when you are
A writer. The only good
Writer's a dead one, it seems.

This morning the clocks
Went back. We gained an hour, but
When we rose, only
Four hours remained before dark.
Sweet and swift, like this, life goes.

Five-forty, Barnehurst
Station. Mist and the smell of
Coal smoke. The setting
For a tale I'll never write—
A brew of dread and magic.

We boarded the train.
A sudden scent recalled those
Days when wishes were
Stars that spiced the night of my
Heart. Was it talcum powder?

A firework's crusty
Burn. The Kingsland Road. It's gone
Midnight. Waiting for
A bus. Mortality. But
The "Bar/Café" sign still shines.

Led Zeppelin's 'Night Flight'.
Hearing it now, I can see
How I've changed. The song
No longer promises new
Blood's Year Zero in my veins.

I am already
Reaping. I have friends, but they
Are distant; honour,
But near secretly; calm, since,
With failure, fatalism.

CPSIA information can be obtained
at www.ICGtesting.com
Printed in the USA
BVOW08s1946200117
474056BV00001B/5/P